HOW TO FIND
MISSING
PERSONS

A Handbook For Investigators

Ronald George Eriksen 2

Loompanics Unlimited
Port Townsend, Washington

Published by:
Loompanics Unlimited
PO Box 1197
Port Townsend, WA 98368

Typesetting and layout by Patrick Michael
Cover by Kevin Martin

ISBN: 0-915179-04-0
Library of Congress Catalog Card Number: 84-80234

CONTENTS

DISCLAIMER

Some of the methods presented in this book may be illegal in some areas of the United States.

Before embarking on any of these schemes, you might want to discuss your plans with your local sheriff or State's Attorney. If you are wealthy, you may wish to consult with a competent attorney, if you can find one.

The author is in no way responsible for the misuse of the information contained in this book.

This book can in no way be used as "proof" of any illegality by the author or his associates.

The author denies that he has ever used any illegal method in this book.

Sold for informational purposes only.

— 1 —

INTRODUCTION

This book will be of value to all types of missing persons investigators. Bounty hunters, private investigators, skip tracers, process servers and auto repossessors, all will learn something new from this manual.

More important, this work will enable the non-professional to locate almost any missing person without paying the often outrageous fees of the investigators mentioned above.

The investigative techniques listed herein don't have to be limited to missing persons cases. For example, the section on tracing license plates will be invaluable to those engaged in surveillance work and the procedures for obtaining telephone records can be adapted to almost any type of investigation.

Using the information contained in this book, you should be able to find just about anybody. In fact, with just a couple weeks' practice you should be able to do a better job than ninety percent of this country's private investigators.

I have tried to write this book as clearly as possible, leaving nothing to the imagination. If after reading this book you have any questions, or any information on the subject you wish to share, feel free to write to me at P.O. Box 8, Buffalo, NY 14212.

It would be greatly appreciated if you enclosed a self-addressed, stamped envelope with your letter.

— 2 —
TYPES OF
MISSING PERSONS

Missing persons can be categorized into separate groups. The specific techniques you would use to find individuals in these groups will vary.

RUNAWAY HUSBANDS AND WIVES

It used to be unheard of for a woman to take off and leave her family behind. Nowadays, it happens all the time. In fact, runaway wives now outnumber runaway husbands.

In these cases, you should concentrate your efforts on the runaway's friends and relatives. The spouse of the runaway should know most of the friends and relatives. Be alert for any signs that the runaway had a boyfriend or girlfriend. If there is one and they have taken off together, it may be easier to find the boyfriend or girlfriend.

One good thing about these cases is that most married couples have joint bank and credit accounts, so obtaining these records should be no problem.

If the runaway has been gone for a while, you would just go down the list of techniques in this book and you should eventually find them. Runaway spouses are almost as easy to find as loan skips.

RUNAWAY KIDS

The missing persons most difficult to locate are runaway kids. Kids can be anywhere and can live in places where even a skid row bum would be too proud to stay. Because of their age, runaway kids are easy prey for pimps and sexual degenerates of various kinds. Also, they do not leave paper trails like adults do.

If you are lucky, maybe one of the kid's friends will have an idea where he or she is. I heard of one investigator who put on a white coat and pretended to be a "doctor." Looking very grim, the investigator told the friends that the runaway had a serious kidney problem and needed special medicine to treat the disorder. The friends were left alone to discuss the matter "privately" among themselves. Of course, the investigator had discreetly placed a $30 wireless microphone nearby to record their conversation. When the discussion was over, they still wouldn't say where the runaway was. However, the investigator now had tape recorded evidence that they knew where he was. This tape recording was played for their parents, who "persuaded" the little brats to talk.

LOAN SKIPS

Loan skips are the easiest to locate and most lucrative type of missing person.

Don't follow the advice of other missing persons books and start looking through city directories and credit reports for these people. These should be among the last things you do.

What you want to do is find as many of them as possible in as short a time as you can. Take a list of skips to your county courthouse and check civil traffic and criminal cases. If it's near a big election and you are in a large city, check the voters registration records, since these are usually kept in the county courthouse also.

Your courthouse research should net you 20-30% of the people you are looking for and you will develop a lot of information about the rest. If you come to the courthouse with a list of 50 names and you find 25% of them, you have found 12 people. If you charge $60 per skip that works out to about $720 for one hour's work. Not too bad.

After going to the courthouse, I would use a telephone ruse on the remaining skips' neighbors, friends and relatives. This should get you another 20%. Then I would check driving records and see what could be found there. This should net you another 20-30%.

For the rest I would then methodically go through the other techniques in this book. By the time you are done you should have found over 90% of the deadbeats and made yourself a tidy sum in the process. Believe me, it's that easy.

ADOPTION CASES

People who are adopted will often pay good money to find their biological parents. Private eyes will charge $3,000 and up for those kinds of investigations.

Assuming you have one of the parents' names (if not, see the chapter on hospital records) most of your work will involve looking through old city directories and phone books for the subject's name. When you find his name you would check the area where he lived, looking for someone from the good old days who remembers the subject. If nobody remembers him, you would then have to skip trace the people who used to live near him.

5

Eventually, you will find someone who remembers that old Henry moved to Bumblebee, Arizona or some such place. If you are lucky you might find enough information about the subject to do a regular skip trace. I know of no investigator who likes to do this kind of investigation. The work is boring and tedious, more like doing library research than an investigation. A very good book on this subject is mentioned in the Recommended Reading section at the back of this book.

CRIMINALS

Criminals can be easy or hard to locate, depending on the individual. Female criminals are harder to locate than their male counterparts due to the greater number of live-in opportunities for them.

Your best bet in these cases is to find out who his friends and relatives are (particularly his sexual partners) and where he hangs out. Then keep an eye on them and wait for him to show up. If he is still in the area, he probably will appear within 24 hours.

To speed things up, you might want to send an off-duty cop or "tough guy" to go and pressure or intimidate the friends and relatives into telling where the subject is. Also, you would want to get their telephone records. Electronic surveillance should be considered, too. Three good books on electronic surveillance are listed in the Recommended Reading section at the back of this book.

Ruses can be effective also. For example, if you are looking for a pimp or prostitute, you could pretend to be a "John" looking to get laid.

— 3 —

FINDING MISSING PERSONS AS A PROFESSION

PRIVATE INVESTIGATORS

The private investigation profession is the most lucrative field involved in the location of missing persons. Private eyes routinely charge $1,000 and up for finding even the easiest to locate people. Most charge at least $100 just to get drivers license information.

The wealthiest P.I.'s hire public relations firms to get their names in the paper every so often. Some even hire writers to write books or magazine articles about them. Such books and articles are filled with exaggerated or even completely fictitious events.

The big problem with this profession is getting in. Most states have ridiculously strict laws governing the P.I. field.

In Illinois, for example, you have to be at least 21 years of age, have no criminal record, and pass a written test. Also, you have to have three years' experience (soon to be five years) in a related field and post a $5,000 bond. It's easier and cheaper to become a lawyer than a private investigator in Illinois.

These strict laws are allegedly set up to "protect the public," but all they really do is restrict competition. The only people who benefit from such laws are the private eyes already in business. In fact, private eye associations hire "lobbyists" to "lobby" politicians into passing even stricter laws.

If you don't qualify for a P.I. license in your state, there are other ways to get into the business.

One way is to go into business with someone who does qualify, such as a retired or ex-cop. This is how most people get around the laws.

Another way is to open a mail drop in a state that has no laws regulating the private eye field. It would also be a good idea to rent a Watts line answering service in another state to answer your calls. (Such answering services cost around $50 per month.) You could then advertise and solicit business in your home state the same way as if you were a licensed private eye.

In such a set up your contact with the public would necessarily have to be by phone or mail. But this is no problem as you rarely have to meet with clients anyway.

The various state bureaucrats have neither the ability nor the inclination to try to enforce their idiotic laws across state lines. Even if they wanted to "get" you, if you had a secure mail drop, what could they do about it? (A book listing hundreds of mail drops in the United States, Canada and other countries is included in the Recommended Reading section at the end of this book.)

PRIVATE PROCESS SERVERS

Private process servers are hired by attorneys to serve legal papers (summonses, subpoenas, etc.) on defendants in civil suits. They are usually paid $25 to $50 for each paper served.

There is no real skill in this business. All you have to do is hand the paper to the defendant. It doesn't matter if he accepts it or not. If he doesn't, all the process server has to do is drop it on the ground and it is considered a legal serve.

The real trick in this business is getting people to admit who they are. The easiest way around this obstacle is to walk up to the defendant's door with a large box addressed to him. Most people are always happy to receive a "present" and when they tell you who they are you hand them the paper.

In this business, you will have people I call "regulars," i.e., people who you serve every other week or so. Most of these regulars will be friendly types and some will even invite you in for a beer. A few, however, will make things difficult for you and will not come to the door when you ring their doorbell. For these, I suggest you use the jury duty scam in the chapter "Finding Out Where Someone Works" to find out where the defendant is employed. If they aren't employed, you might send an "hysterical crying female" to the door, saying she just plowed into the defendant's car. When he comes out to inspect the "damage," you or the crying female can nail him with the paper.

If these tricks are unsuccessful, then call up the local police department and tell them that you have a summons for the defendant and he won't come to the door. Ask them to send a squad car out and charge him with "obstruction of civil process." (Believe it or not, there is such a law in nearly every state.) A very few police departments will be reluctant to do this, but even these will at least send someone to knock on the door. This will usually scare the defendant into coming to the door.

Most police officers, particularly big city cops, will do a lot more than bang on the door, however. I have had police officers actually break down the door of a person's residence so that I could serve a summons. One gung-ho Chicago cop actually got an ax and threatened to break down the door of a telephone company that refused to let me in to serve one of their employees. They let us in.

Whenever serving a summons in a slum area or housing project, always get a police escort. If you go in alone to these places, you are insane. I have never been refused a police escort in a bad neighborhood.

RUNNING A PROCESS SERVING BUSINESS

You can operate this business from your house or apartment. For advertising, you can send some inexpensive flyers out to every attorney in your area. You might also want to place a small ad in your local law journal.

Your skip tracing skills will come in handy for stealing business from competitors. Almost all private process servers are ignorant about skip tracing. To steal business from them, go to your county courthouse and look at the civil files plaintiff index. Try to find a company that has sued a lot of people. Write down all the case numbers and obtain the files of every case the company has been involved with. When looking through these files, you will come across cases where the process server has been unable to serve the defendant. This is almost always because the defendant has moved and neither the process server nor the attorney handling the case have any idea where he has gone. The strategy here is to locate the defendant yourself and then call the attorney and tell him that you know the defendant's new address and, if he gives you the paper, you can serve him. After you have successfully served the defendant, point out how much better you are than the other process server. If he is profit oriented (and most attorneys are) he will start giving you papers on a regular basis.

There are a few bad points to mention about the process serving business. First of all, it's pretty boring work. Second, you drive around a lot, putting a lot of wear and tear on your car. And third, you have to deal with attorneys, many of whom seem to have difficulty paying their bills.

Still, you can make good money in this business. $75,000 a year is not unusual for a good process server.

BOUNTY HUNTERS

Bounty hunters track down bailjumpers for bailbondsmen. They usually earn 20-50% of the subject's bond.

When a bailjumper skips town, the bailbondsman becomes liable for the entire bond. In most states, the bailbondsman is given a certain amount of time to bring the bailjumper back into custody before forfeiting the bond. In California, this time period is 180 days, while in Utah it is only 14 days. Even in states where little or no time is given to bring the bailjumper back, the judge handling the case will generally be reasonable and will grant a certain amount of time to apprehend the bailjumper.

When a person is bailed out of jail by a bailbondsman, that person is released into the custody of the bondsman. If that person then skips town, the bailbondsman and his agents (bounty hunters) have the absolute right to bring him into custody. The U.S. Supreme Court and

11

numerous state courts are very clear on this matter. In Taylor vs. Taintor, 16 Wall 366 (21 Law Ed. 287) the Supreme Court of the U.S. ruled:

> When bail is given, the principal is regarded as delivered to the custody of his sureties. Their dominion is a continuance of the original imprisonment. Whenever they choose to do so, they may seize and deliver up in their discharge, and if that cannot be done at once, they may imprison him until it can be done. They may exercise their rights in person or by agent. They may pursue him into another state, may arrest him on the sabbath, and if necessary, may break and enter his house for that purpose. The seizure is not made by virtue of new process. None is needed.

This work is nothing like what TV bounty hunters do. Instead of jumping off trains chasing after a large-busted blonde, you will probably be looking through skid row flophouses searching for a 300 lb. ex-prostitute.

The work is dangerous, too. Most bailjumpers will do anything and everything to stay out of jail. One bounty hunter friend of mine was kicked in the "groin" by the 300 lb. ex-hooker mentioned earlier. The kick was of such force that it broke every blood vessel in that very sensitive area of his anatomy. It hurts just thinking about it.

Much of what was written in the section on chasing down criminals is relevant to the bounty hunter profession. One thing that might be added is when you apprehend a bailjumper try to treat him with respect. Maybe you can give him a cigaret or a stiff drink or something. When he gets back on the streets again, he will remember your kindness and may be willing to help you on another case.

To get into this profession, you would want to contact bailbondsmen and insurance companies that write bonds. Even if they already have a bounty hunter, they probably have a lot of cases outstanding which are costing them a lot of money.

— 4 —

ARREST RECORDS

Arrest records in and of themselves are of limited value in missing person cases. They are probably worth obtaining only in lucrative cases, or those cases in which you are personally involved.

If the case is important and if it appears that the subject of your search may have been involved in some kind of criminal activity, then it may be a good idea to obtain the arrest records.

Once you obtain these records you would then contact arresting officers, probation officers, prosecuting attorneys, defense attorneys, accomplices, and victims to see if they have any information concerning the subject's whereabouts.

There are several methods of obtaining arrest records.

POLICE INFORMANTS

It is not very hard to find an informant in a police agency. If you own your own investigative firm or process service business, you can put an ad in the paper for part time help. Specify in the ad that you want police officers as potential employees. When one applies for the job, give him some summonses to serve or put him on a routine investigation of some sort. After a few weeks of feeling him out and getting to know him, ask him to run some drivers license checks for you. If he goes for this (and he probably will) he will probably be willing to obtain arrest records for you.

Another way to find a police informant is to shoot regularly at shooting ranges. You will find many police types at such places. It should be fairly easy to make friends with them. Many law enforcement people will run an arrest record check for free with no strings attached if the individual you are looking for is a low-life person.

BAILBONDSMEN

If the person you are looking for has ever been bailed out of jail by a bailbondsman, you can be sure that the bailbondsman has a record of it. The strategy here is to pretend to be a bailbondsman yourself. Call up every bailbondsman in each city where the subject has lived. Tell each one that the subject has used him as a reference and ask what offense the subject was bailed out for. Most bailbondsmen will be happy to give you the information.

CHURCH LEAGUE OF AMERICA

If the subject has ever been involved in "anti-American" activities, he might be listed in the files of the Church League of America.

This tax-exempt outfit has millions of files on individuals and organizations involved in left wing political activity of all kinds. You can get four names checked for a "contribution" of $132.50. Their address is Church League of America, 422 North Prospect, Wheaton, IL 60187.

NEWSPAPERS

If the subject has ever been arrested for a felony, there is a good chance the local newspaper has a record of it. Most papers keep a "morgue" of back issues either at their office or at the library on microfiche. Many keep an index to these files also.

COUNTY COURTHOUSES

Your local county courthouse has records of all people charged with crimes in the county. For information on how to access these records, see the chapter on Courthouse Records.

— 5 —

BANKS

Copies of the subject's cancelled checks could give you clues to his location. He may have paid for airline tickets with a check, or maybe he made a check out to a friend who knows where he is.

These records are not as hard to obtain as you might think. Bankers are not well known for their discretion in these matters and any friend in the banking or brokerage business can get you the needed information.

How do you find such friends? This is where the credit reporting companies come in handy. Sooner or later you will locate someone who a bank is looking for in an entirely different matter. The credit report will show if he is a skip or not. If he is, call the bank and tell them you have found their man. This will gain you many friends at that bank.

I once found a woman who had skipped on a $60,000 bank loan. Needless to say, the bank was very pleased that I had found her. From that day on the bank was always there to help me with "special favors."

BANK RUSE

Banks may be in possession of information on the subject that could help you in your search. Here is how

17

one operative who doesn't have banking contacts obtains the desired information over the phone.

Bank: Good afternoon, First National Bank of Flagstaff.

Operative: Bookkeeping please.

Bank: One moment please. *Pause...*

Bank: Bookkeeping.

Operative: Hi, this is Bob Bozo over at the Lincoln Bank. We're having some check kiting problems involving a Ramona Shyster, date of birth 6-06-56. We put her through the T.R.W. and the only thing that came back was your bank. Could you check your records and see what address you have her at?

Bank: Sure, hold on a minute. *Pause...*

Bank: We've got her at 2020 Deadbeat Road here in Flagstaff.

Operative: Yeah, that's where I've got her, too. Does it say where she's employed?

Bank: She's a paper hanger at Ponzi's Paper Hanging here in Flagstaff.

Operative: Thank you very much. This should help a lot.

FINDING OUT WHERE SOMEONE BANKS

The following two ruses are used on the subject to determine where he banks. Attorneys and creditors are always anxious to find out this information. You'll need to know the subject's telephone number for these ruses.

Operative: Ramona Shyster, please.

Subject: Yeah.

Operative: Miss Shyster, this is Bob Bozo over at the Collection Department of Mountain Bell. The reason I'm calling, Miss Shyster, is to inform you that service will be discontinued on June first unless we receive payment in full by that date.

Subject: What? What kind of bullshit is this? I paid that bill two weeks ago. What the hell is going on?

Operative: When was the check made out, and at what bank do you have your checking account?

Subject: Oh, shit, I don't know exactly when it was made out. My account is with the First National Bank of Phoenix, though.

Operative: Okay, hold on a minute while I put this information through our computer. *Pause..*

Operative: All right, Miss Shyster, everything has been taken care of. Service will not be discontinued and I'm sorry to have bothered you about this.

Subject: Yeah, all right.

BANK SOLICITATION RUSE

Operative: Ramona Shyster, please.

Subject: Yeah?

Operative: Ramona, this is Bob Bozo over at the First Federal Bank downtown. We're calling to tell you that our bank is now offering free checking accounts to all new depositors who open a savings account with a minimum balance of five hundred dollars. Would you be interested in opening an account with us?

Subject: No, I'm sorry, I'm not interested.

Operative: Well, where do you bank at now?

Subject: I bank at the Lincoln Bank.

Operative: Thank you for your time, Miss Shyster.

IN THE MAIL

Yet another way to find out where someone banks is to send them a check from your personal or business account. When your cancelled check comes back in the mail in a month or so, just look on the back of the check and it will say what bank he cashed it at.

When sending the check, you might want to type a letter on a business letterhead, saying he overpaid you for some type of service, and that you are sending him his refund of $5.

The bum you send it to will believe he has come onto a windfall and will run to the bank to cash his ill-gotten gains.

SUBPOENAS

A very effective way to gain access to someone's bank records is to file a $31 lawsuit against the subject and subpoena his bank records. Subpoenas are issued without any questions by the County Clerk's office.

SWISS BANKS

I was once hired to prove that someone had a bank account in Switzerland. It was a divorce case and the wife knew that her husband had a large account with a certain bank in Switzerland. He, of course, denied it, and the bank refused to provide any information at all. Here is how I obtained the necessary proof.

First, I wrote to the bank telling them I wanted to open an account with them. They sent me an application form on which the only identifying information asked for was my full name, date of birth and passport number. I then thought up a ruse and called the bank, secretly tape-recording the conversation. The spiel went something like this:

Swiss Bank: Good afternoon, Swiss Bank (*speaking in German*).

Operative: Hello, this is Larry Launder calling from the United States (*speaking in English*).

Swiss Bank: One minute, please (*speaking in German*), *Pause...*

Swiss Bank: Can I help you? This is Miss Guzunteit (*now speaking in English*).

Operative: Yes, this is Larry Launder calling from the U.S.A. I've just learned that my wife has forged my signature on a letter and requested that all the funds in my account at your bank be sent to her. Has her letter arrived yet? You didn't send her the money, did you?

Swiss Bank: What is your account number, Mr. Launder?

Operative: I don't know. My financial papers are in a safe deposit box in New York. I'm in Chicago now.

Swiss Bank: Do you have any information with which to identify yourself, Mr. Launder?

Operative: Well, I was born December 7, 1940.

Swiss Bank: One minute please, Mr. Launder. *Pause...*

Swiss Bank: Mr. Launder, we have received no communication regarding your account since July. No money has been transferred in that time either.

Operative: Oh, that's a relief. Then my money is still safe and secure in your bank?

Swiss Bank: Yes it is, Mr. Launder. We will need you to fill out a new signature card, however.

Operative: Of course. Please send it to me immediately.

Swiss Bank: We will send it today.

Operative: Thank you. Goodbye.

All the above actually happened. I was amazed at how easy the Swiss Bank was bamboozled. (The above is not *exactly* what was said. It was a 15 minute conversation, but the main points were very similar to the above.)

— 6 —

COURTHOUSE RECORDS

There is an incredible amount of information contained in the records at your county courthouse.

For our purposes, the most important of these records are traffic, criminal, and civil records.

The indexes to traffic and criminal cases are usually kept in the same book or microfiche card. These records are supposed to be public information, but in large cities, the clerks handling these things often will deny you access to these files. A call to the local Bar Association or State Attorney's office will prod these pointy-headed bureaucrats into obeying the law. Another way to handle this type of situation is to bring a tape recorder and a copy of your state's freedom of information law to the courthouse. Show the law to the bureaucrat and with the tape recorder on ask the "public servant" on what grounds he is denying you access to the records. This should result in the bureaucrat melting away before your eyes just like the Wicked Witch of Oz.

In examining traffic records, be sure to check what address the defendant gave the traffic cop. In many cases it will be different from what is on his drivers license. Also, if the fine was paid by mail, there might be a copy of the check and the envelope he used to send it in. Check both, because there might be a different address on these also.

In criminal cases, always check to see where the defendant was served legal papers, his probation officer if he was convicted, and all details of the crime, such as witnesses, victims, arresting officers, etc. Any of these may lead you to the current location of the person you are looking for.

Civil records include divorce, personal injury, collection, and other non-criminal matters. When checking these, be sure to see where the defendant was served legal papers, the address on the complaint, the plaintiff, the defendant's attorney, and any other item in the file that might help you in your search.

Civil cases sometimes show who some of the subject's enemies are. For example, in a divorce case the two parties will often sling a lot of mud at each other.

— 7 —

CREDIT BUREAUS

An overrated method of locating missing persons is through credit reports put out by various credit bureaus. I have found that information from such credit reports is often outdated and inaccurate. Also, the information does not cross state lines; that is, if you check on someone's credit record in Illinois, it will not show anything about his dealings in California. You have to ask and pay for a separate credit check if you want his records there.

Skip tracers employed by collection agencies spend their days talking with companies mentioned on a deadbeat's credit report, hoping to find out where the deadbeat has gone to. These collection agency skip tracers find only about three people a day doing things this way. My experience has been that when someone skips town, they usually skip on *all* their creditors, not just a few.

About the only value I have found in using these reports and contacting the companies on them is that you might find information about the skip that you didn't know. Maybe the credit report mentions an old address of the skip's that you didn't know about. Or maybe one of the companies mentioned on the report knows a relative that you didn't know of.

If you want these records, you don't need an informant to get them. Anybody with a "legitimate business purpose" can gain access to them. All you have to do is pay the annual membership fee — usually around $50 per year. Accounts with these credit bureaus can even be opened over the phone.

The only two credit bureaus worth subscribing to are T.R.W. and Trans-Union. All the others are a joke and even these two leave a lot to be desired.

— 8 —

CREDIT CARD RECORDS

These are very valuable records, particularly for hard core skips. Credit card records show where and when the subject bought a particular piece of merchandise. I know of no pretext that can be used to obtain these records. A telephone ruse has been used to obtain the subject's last known address from the credit card companies. You have to know the subject's credit card number, his date of birth, and a couple of his previous addresses. What you do is call the credit card company and tell them "you" are declaring bankruptcy and want to know how much "you" owe them. When they tell you how much you owe, you would say something like "Gee, I don't recall receiving a bill for that. What address did you send it to?" Usually they will give it to you, but sometimes they will ask for your date of birth and a couple of prior addresses so they can make sure it's really you.

Many investigators have managed to become members of an organization called the International Association of Credit Card Investigators, 1620 Grant Avenue, Novato, CA 94947. By joining this organization and participating in its meetings and social functions, you should be able to find contacts in the major credit card companies. Only a perfunctory check is made on potential members.

— 9 —
DRIVERS
LICENSE RECORDS

Contrary to what the police and private investigators might tell you, driving records are public information and anybody can obtain them in all states except Arkansas, North Carolina, Pennsylvania and Wisconsin.

Among other things, these records can tell you where and when the subject has been stopped for a moving violation and his current address. You should contact every state in which the subject is likely to be. Of course, you would start with the state in which he most recently lived. If you have no luck here, you would then write to the states where he was born, where he received his social security number, all states where he previously lived and vacationed, and finally, all warm weather states.

Listed below are the addresses and fees of the state agencies to contact when you want copies of anyone's driving record. When writing for these records, request an abstract of the subject's driving record. You should include the subject's full name and date of birth and the necessary fee. A few states have forms which are to be filled out when requesting these records. Except for the four states mentioned previously, you don't really need to use the forms if you make only infrequent requests.

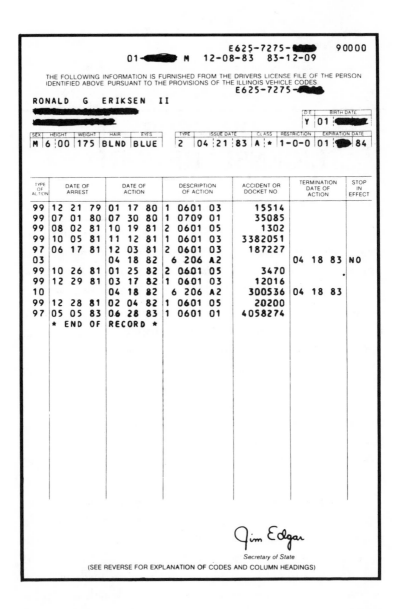

A typical abstract of the subject's license records.

LIDR-1 (Rev. 3/75)

REQUEST FOR INFORMATION FROM TEXAS DRIVER LICENSING RECORDS

(MAIL TO: License Issuance & Driver Records, Texas Department of Public Safety, Box 4087, Austin, Texas 78773)

TO BE COMPLETED BY PERSON REQUESTING INFORMATION

INFORMATION REQUESTED ON: (Type or print)

DRIVER LICENSE NUMBER (as shown on Driver License)

CHECK TYPE SERVICE DESIRED

☐ 1 Date of birth-License status-Latest address. Fee $0.25
☐ 2 Sum total of accidents and violations in record itemized by date and location within immediate past three year period. Fee $0.75
☐ 3 Date of birth-License status-Latest address-List of reported violations and accidents contained in record. Fee $1.00

LAST NAME   FIRST   MIDDLE OR MAIDEN

DATE OF BIRTH
Month   Day   Year

COMPLETED BY DPS

For Department of Public Safety Accounting Control

REQUESTED BY   (Name of Person or Firm)

MAILING ADDRESS   STREET/BOX NUMBER

CITY   STATE   ZIP CODE

A typical form which some states require when writing for a subject's driving record.

31

ALABAMA
Drivers License Division
Certification Section
PO Box 1471
Montgomery, Alabama 36102
(205) 832-5100
Fee: $2.00

ALASKA
Dept. of Public Safety
Drivers License Section
Pouch N
Juneau, Alaska 99801
(907) 465-4396
Fee: $2.00

ARIZONA
Motor Vehicle Division
1801 W. Jefferson Street
Phoenix, Arizona 85007
(602) 255-7011
Fee: Record check — $2.00
    Current Address — $2.00

ARKANSAS
Office of Driver Services
Traffic Violation Report Unit
PO Box 1272
Little Rock, Arkansas 72203
(501) 371-1671
Fee: $5.00
Write for required form

CALIFORNIA
Dept. of Motor Vehicles
PO Box 11231
Sacramento, California 95813
(916) 445-4568
Fee: $0.75
Write for required form

COLORADO
Dept. of Revenue
Motor Vehicle Division
Master File Section
140 W. Sixth Avenue
Denver, Colorado 80204
(303) 892-3407
Fee: $1.25

CONNECTICUT
Dept. of Motor Vehicles
Copy Record Section
60 State Street
Wethersfield, Connecticut 06109
(203) 566-2638
Fee: $4.00

DELAWARE
Motor Vehicle Department
PO Box 698
Dover, Delaware 19901
(302) 736-4760
Fee: $2.00

DISTRICT OF COLUMBIA
Dept. of Transportation
Bureau of Motor Vehicles

301 C. Street, N.W.
Washington, D.C.
(202) 727-6680
Fee: $0.50

FLORIDA
Drivers License Division
Dept. of Highway Safety
Kirkham Building
Tallahassee, Florida 323~~1~~
(904) ~~488-9145~~
Fee: $3.00
Write for required form

GEORGIA
Dept. of Public Safety
Drivers Service Section
Merit Rating
PO Box 1456
Atlanta, Georgia 30301
(404) 656-2339
Fee: $2.00

HAWAII
District of The First Circuit
Violations Bureau
842 Bethel Street
Honolulu, Hawaii 96813
(808) 548-5735
Fee: $1.00

IDAHO
Dept. of Law Enforcement
Motor Vehicle Division

PO Box 34
Boise, Idaho 83731
(208) 334-3650
Fee: $1.50

ILLINOIS
Secretary of State
Drivers Services Dept.
Driver Analysis Section
2701 S. Dirksen Parkway
Springfield, Illinois 62723
(217) 782-3720
Fee: $2.00
Write for required form

INDIANA
Bureau of Motor Vehicles
Paid Mail Section
Room 416, State Office Building
Indianapolis, Indiana 46204
(317) 232-2798
Fee: $1.00

IOWA
Dept. of Transportation
Records Section
Lucas Building
Des Moines, Iowa 50319
(515) 281-5656
Fee: $1.00

KANSAS
Division of Vehicles
Driver Control Bureau

State Office Building
Topeka, Kansas 66626
(913) 296-3671
Fee: $1.00

KENTUCKY
Division of Driver Licensing
New State Office Building
Frankfort, Kentucky 40601
(502) 564-6800
Fee: $2.00

LOUISIANA
Dept. of Public Safety
Drivers License Division
O.D.R. Section, Box 1271
Baton Rouge, Louisiana 70821
(504) 925-6343
Fee: $2.00

MAINE
Secretary of State
Motor Vehicle Division
1 Child Street
Augusta, Maine 04333
(207) 289-2761
Fee: $3.00

MASSACHUSETTS
Registry of Motor Vehicles
Court Records Section
100 Nashua Street
Boston, Massachusetts 02114
(617) 727-3842
Fee: $3.00

MICHIGAN
Dept. of State
Bureau of Driver and Vehicle Services
Commercial Look-Up Unit
7064 Crowner Drive
Lansing, Michigan 48918
(517) 322-1460
Fee: $5.00

MINNESOTA
Dept. of Public Safety
Drivers License Office
Room 108, State Highway Building
St. Paul, Minnesota 55155
(612) 296-6911
Fee: $2.00
Write for required form

MISSISSIPPI
Mississippi Highway Safety Patrol
Drivers License Issuance Board
PO Box 958
Jackson, Mississippi 39205
(601) 987-1236
Fee: $3.50

MISSOURI
Bureau of Drivers License
Dept. of Revenue
PO Box 200
Jefferson City, Missouri 65101
(314) 751-4600
Fee: $1.00

MONTANA
Montana Highway Patrol
303 Roberts
Helena, Montana 59601
(406) 449-3000
Fee: $2.00

NEBRASKA
Dept. of Motor Vehicles
Drivers Records Section
PO Box 94789
Lincoln, Nebraska 68509
(402) 471-2281
Fee: $0.75

NEVADA
CBM of Nevada

PO Box 1964
Carson City, Nevada 89701
(702) 885-5360
Fee: $1.25

NEW HAMPSHIRE
Division of Motor Vehicles
Driver Record Research Unit
85 Loudon Road
Concord, New Hampshire 03301
(603) 271-2371
Fee: $5.00

NEW JERSEY
Division of Motor Vehicles
Bureau of Security Responsibility

25 S. Montgomery Street
Trenton, New Jersey 08666
(609) 292-7500
Fee: $5.00

NEW MEXICO
Transportation Dept.
Driver Services Bureau
Manuel Lujan Sr. Building
Santa Fe, New Mexico 87503
(505) 827-7522
Fee: $1.10

NEW YORK
Dept. of Motor Vehicles
Public Service Bureau
Empire State Plaza
Albany, New York 12228
(518) 473-5595
Fee: $2.00

NORTH CAROLINA
Traffic Records Section
Division of Motor Vehicles
Raleigh, North Carolina 27611
(919) 733-4241
Fee: $1.00
Write for required form

NORTH DAKOTA
Drivers License Division
Capitol Grounds
Bismarck, North Dakota 58505
(701) 224-2600
Fee: $2.00

OHIO
Bureau of Motor Vehicles
PO Box 16520
Columbus, Ohio 43216
(614) 863-7500
Fee: $1.00

OKLAHOMA
Driver Records Service
Dept. of Public Safety
PO Box 11415
Oklahoma City, Oklahoma 73136
(405) 424-4011
Fee: $3.00

OREGON
Motor Vehicles Division
1905 Lona Avenue
Salem, Oregon 97314
(503) 371-2200
Fee: $6.00

PENNSYLVANIA
Dept. of Transportation
Bureau of Accident Analysis
Operator Information Section
Room 212
Transportation and Safety Building
Harrisburg, Pennsylvania 17120
(717) 783-6605
Fee: $1.50
Write for required form

RHODE ISLAND
Registry of Motor Vehicles
Room 101G
State Office Building
Providence, Rhode Island 02903
(401) 277-2970
Fee: $1.50

SOUTH CAROLINA
Dept. of Highways and Public Transportation
Driver Record Check Section, Room 201
Columbia, South Carolina 29216
(605) 758-2125
Fee: $3.00

SOUTH DAKOTA
Dept. of Public Safety
Driver Improvement Program
118 W. Capitol
Pierre, South Dakota 57501
(605) 773-3191
Fee: $2.00
Write for required form

TENNESSEE
Dept. of Safety
Jackson Building
Nashville, Tennessee 37219
(615) 741-3954
Fee: $3.00

TEXAS
Dept. of Public Safety
License Issuance and Driver Records

PO Box 4087
Austin, Texas 78773
(512) 465-2000
Fee: $1.00
Write for required form

UTAH
Drivers License Division
314 State Office Building
Salt Lake City, Utah 84114
(801) 965-4400
Fee: $1.00

VERMONT
Agency of Transportation
Dept. of Motor Vehicles
Montpelier, Vermont 05602
(802) 828-2121
Fee: $3.00

VIRGINIA
Division of Motor Vehicles
Driver Licensing and Information Dept.
PO Box 27412
Richmond, Virginia 23269
(804) 257-0538
Fee: $3.00

WASHINGTON
Division of Licensing
Dept. of Motor Vehicles
Olympia, Washington 98501
(206) 753-6969
Fee: $1.50

WEST VIRGINIA
Driver Improvement Division
Dept. of Motor Vehicles
1800 Washington Street, East
Charleston, West Virginia 25305
(304) 348-3900
Fee: $1.00

WISCONSIN
Dept. of Transportation
Driver Record File
PO Box 7918
Madison, Wisconsin 53707
(608) 266-2261
Fee: $1.00
Write for required form

WYOMING
Dept. of Revenue
2200 Carey Avenue
Cheyenne, Wyoming 82001
(307) 777-6516
Fee: $1.00

RUSES

Sometimes you may need drivers license information in a hurry rather than waiting the two weeks or so it takes to receive it by mail.

What follows is a hypothetical transcript of an operative using a telephone ruse to obtain the drivers license address of the person he is looking for. In this case the operative is calling the county sheriff.

Sheriff: Sheriff's office, Fife speaking.

Operative: Yeah hi, this is Bob Bozo over at the State Attorney's office. Our line with Phoenix is down. Can you run a twenty-seven for us? (*A twenty-seven in police lingo is a drivers license readout, a twenty-eight is a license plate readout.*)

Sheriff: Sure, Bob. What's the license number?

Operative: We don't have the license number. We have the date of birth though.

Sheriff: That's good enough. What's the last name?

Operative: Cojones, and that's spelled C-o-j-o-n-e-s.

Sheriff: First name?

Operative: Carlos.

Sheriff: Middle initial?

Operative: A.

Sheriff: Date of birth?

Operative: June 6, 1956.

Sheriff: Okay, hold on a minute, Bob, and I'll put it through. *Pause...*

Sheriff: Okay, what did you need to know?

Operative: Is there a stop in effect? (*A stop is a license suspension.*)

Sheriff: No.

Operative: What's his address?

Sheriff: Route 3, Box 395, Gila Bend.

Operative: Thanks a lot.

This ruse works nine times out of ten. You don't have to call the local sheriff if you don't want to. Anyone with a computer hookup to the state drivers license division can get you the information. For example, many forest ranger and local drivers license facilities have them. These people are often easier than the sheriff.

This ruse will also work on the bureaucrats at the drivers license headquarters in your state's capitol city. Experience has proven that if you have a police scanner going in the background when you call the state bureaucrats, your odds for getting the information will increase to nearly 100%.

Whenever using the above ruse, always be friendly and try to "shoot the bull" with the bureaucrat or sheriff. Then you can call back again and again and get information.

A few states (California, for example) will ask you for your code name when you call. When this happened to the above operative, he replied that he just had the name in front of him but that he had lost it. He was then asked what office he was with, to which he replied, "With the State Attorney's office" in the county where he lived. He was then informed that his code name was "Fox Bat 23." Now, whenever he needs drivers license information, he simply calls up the state headquarters and gives "his" code name and obtains all the information he needs with no problems.

Another way to obtain the code name is through the following telephone ruse.

Sheriff: Sheriff's office, Fife speaking.

Operative: Hi, this is Bob Bozo calling from the Secretary of State's Office in Phoenix. We're calling just to make sure you have the new code name. What code name do you have?

Sheriff: Let me see; hold on a minute. Here it is. "Gemini" is the code name we have. Is that the right one?

Operative: Oh, so you do have it. Yes, that's the one. Sorry to have bothered you.

Sheriff: No problem. Good-bye.

LAZY MAN'S RUSE

For you lazy people out there who don't want to work or think too hard, I have developed the "lazy man's ruse." In this ruse, you simply call up your state drivers license headquarters and pretend to be the person whose record you want. Let's see how it works.

Secretary of State: Secretary of State's office. Can I help you?

Operative: Yeah, this is Jack Ripper in Huntsville. My wife just called me and said we received a letter from you saying my license is being suspended. Can you check and find out why?

Secretary of State: Sure, Mr. Ripper. What's your full name and date of birth?

Operative: Jack T. Ripper and I was born December 7, 1941.

Secretary of State: Okay, hold on a minute, Mr. Ripper, while I put this through. *Pause...*

Secretary of State: Mr. Ripper, I just put your name through our computer and it came out clean — not a single violation. Are you sure the letter said your license was being suspended?

Operative: Yeah, I'm sure. Maybe you sent it to the wrong Jack Ripper. What address do you have me at?

Secretary of State: We have you at 100 Lovers Lane, Huntsville.

Operative: Yeah, that's me. It must be a mixup or something. Good-bye.

This ruse has failed only once, and even then the operative learned that the person he was looking for had a license in that state. Also, it can be used for "fishing expeditions," i.e., calling various states to find out if someone has a license there.

TRANSFERRED AND EXPIRED LICENSES

If someone's license has long expired and there is no mention on the abstract of it being transferred to another state, then there is a good chance that the person has moved to Texas. For some reason, Texas does not notify a licensee's old state that he has gotten a license there.

MICROFICHE

In most states, the drivers license headquarters keeps a microfiche section where they keep records of deceased drivers, old expired licenses, and old records showing which state a drivers license has been transferred to.

Tell the people in the microfiche section that you are with your local state attorney's office and that you have a grand jury summons for the person you are looking for. This scam has proven successful for many operatives.

ADDRESS VERIFICATION

Some states have a free service whereby you call them up and give them a name, date of birth, and an address and they will tell you if the address is the one they have in their records. This service is used mainly by auto rental agencies. It, too, can be used for "fishing expeditions."

COMPANIES

Listed below are two companies that can obtain drivers license information for you. I have never used either of them. After reading this chapter, you won't need to use them either.

Data Research, Inc.
3600 American River Drive
Sacramento, CA 95825
(916) 485-3282
(800) 824-8806

V.O.S.
P.O. Box 15334
Sacramento, CA 95813
(916) 451-8475

— 10 —

EX-NEIGHBORS

There are many people who have nothing better to do with their time than to keep an eye on their neighbors. These are the type of people you are looking for. Often, these people will be most anxious to reveal all the dirty details of the subject's sordid past to anyone who asks.

You don't have to spend time and money visiting the ex-neighbors in person. You can find out who they are by looking them up in your local city directory and then calling them on the phone. A scam that has proven very successful on ex-neighbors is the "loan officer" ruse. Here's how it goes:

Operative: Wanda Wolfe, please.

Ex-Neighbor: Speaking.

Operative: Hi, Mrs. Wolfe, this is Bob Bozo over at A.B.C. Financial Services. Linda Lobo has given your name as a reference on a loan application. Do you have a minute to answer a few questions?

Ex-Neighbor: Sure.

Operative: How long have you known the applicant?

Ex-Neighbor: Uh, let's see now. Uh, five years.

Operative: And how long has she lived in the area?

Ex-Neighbor: Oh, I don't know. I think she was born here.

Operative: Where is she currently employed?

Ex-Neighbor: She works at the Tom Cat Lounge on Route thirty-eight.

Operative: Finally, Mrs. Wolfe, what is Linda's current address to the best of your knowledge?

Ex-Neighbor: She's now living in the Norwegian Woods Apartments in Tempe.

Operative: Okay, thank you very much, Mrs. Wolfe.

IN PERSON

The "package" ruse and the "old friend" routine mentioned in the Friends and Relatives chapter will work equally well on ex-neighbors. When talking to these people always ask how the subject moved out of his place. Did he hire a mover? Or did he move himself? If he moved himself, did he make several trips on the same day moving things? If so, he is obviously still in the area.

When talking to the ex-neighbors, always be alert for any hostility they might have for the person you are looking for. If such hostility is exhibited, tell them who you really are (process server, repo man, etc.) and they will usually help you as best they can.

Ex-neighbors usually know *something* that would aid you in your search. Maybe they know a relative that you don't know about. Or maybe they know what bar he hung out at. It's often worthwhile to visit these people in person if talking to them on the telephone did not get you the desired information.

— 11 —

FINDING OUT WHERE SOMEONE WORKS

Attorneys and creditors are always interested in where deadbeats work. This is so they can garnish their wages.

Experience has proven that the easiest way to acquire this information is through the infamous "jury duty" telephone ruse. Here's how it goes.

Operative: Leroy Brown, please.

Subject: This is him.

Operative: Hi, Mr. Brown, this is Bob Bozo over at the Cook County Commissioner's office. The reason I'm calling is that your name had come up for jury duty during the month of January. We sent some forms out there for you to fill out, but we never got them back. Did you actually receive them?

Subject: No, I didn't receive no forms.

Operative: Okay, I'll fill them out now for you. We only have a few preliminary questions. First, are you handicapped in any way that would require special facilities?

Subject: No.

Operative: Are there any children whose care would prevent you from serving on jury duty?

Subject: No.

Operative: Have you ever been convicted of a felony?

Subject: No.

Operative: Where are you currently employed?

Subject: I work at Motorola in Cicero.

Operative: Okay, one more thing, Mr. Brown. The fee that you are to receive for appearing on jury duty is deposited directly into your bank. Do you have a preference as to what bank you would like the funds deposited in?

Subject: Well, my checking account is with the First National Bank in Cicero.

Operative: Thank you, Mr. Brown.

Once in a while when using this ruse someone will say, "How did you get my name for jury duty? I'm not registered to vote." For this, tell the wise guy that your state gets its names from drivers licenses, tax scrolls, telephone directories and the Census Bureau.

Sometimes, people will not want to appear for jury duty and will say things like, "I ain't servin' on no jury duty." For this, tell the reluctant person that they don't have to appear if they have a good reason, but they still have to give you the information.

The "jury duty" ruse is one of the all-time favorites. It works 99.9% of the time. It gets everybody. Try it and see for yourself.

12

FRIENDS AND RELATIVES

The friends and relatives of the person you are looking for almost always have at least some idea as to where he is.

These people are usually (but not always) very loyal to the subject and will not give you any information unless you use deception. The telephone ruse below is an example of the type of deception you are going to have to use.

DOCTOR RUSE

Operative: Sally Smith, please.

Relative: This is she.

Operative: Miss Smith, this is Dr. Noe over at the emergency room at St. Edward's Hospital. We have a child belonging to Ramona Shyster over here, and it is very important that we get in touch with her. Do you have any idea where she may be?

Relative: Oh my god! That must be my nephew. Is it Michael? Is he alright? What happened?

Operative: Yes, it is Michael. He had a close

call with a truck, but he's fine — not a mark on him. We just can't release him until a relative comes and picks him up. Do you know where Miss Shyster is?

Relative: Oh, thank god. Let's see, my sister should be at work now. She works at the First National Bank of Phoenix. Do you want me to call her?

Operative: No, we'll handle it over here. Thank you very much for the information. Good-bye.

Caution! Relatives of the subject may become hysterical when you use this ruse. If the relative is a female, you might want to use a different scam such as the loan officer ruse in the chapter on Ex-Neighbors. Unless it's an important case, there's no reason to upset an innocent person.

IN PERSON

Two "in person" ruses which have proven very successful on relatives are the "package" ruse and the "old friend" ruse.

In the "package" ruse, you appear at the home of the subject's relative with a large box addressed to the subject. Of course, the package must be signed for personally by the subject. When the person at the door tells you that the subject has moved, you would then ask for a forwarding address.

The "old friend" ruse takes more skill than the "package" routine. In this scam, you would visit the subject's relative and ask for the subject by his first name. During the ensuing conversation you would ask where the subject now lives, works, etc.

Some in person ruses can be truly bizarre. For example, I know of an investigator who passed as a Catholic priest in order to obtain information in a Mexican neighborhood.

MAIL RUSES

One mail ruse that has been very successful is the bogus employment offer.

A letter offering a fantastic job opportunity is sent to the subject at a relative's address. An employment application is also enclosed. A typical job application form will ask where the subject lives and works. Some custom-made ones I have seen ask for a banking reference.

Keep trying to get information from the relatives. If one relative won't help, maybe another one will. Call at different times of the day or night. If that doesn't work, go there in person or use a mail ruse. Maybe you can enlist the help of a friend or neighbor of the relative to get the desired information.

Don't give up easily on the relatives. These people almost always are in possession of valuable information concerning the subject.

— 13 —

HOSPITAL RECORDS

Once in a while you will find out that the person you are looking for just got out of the hospital. The hospital probably has his new address, but of course such information is considered "confidential."

Perhaps the best way to obtain this confidential information is through a telephone ruse. Call up the hospital having the records you want and ask for "Medical Records." After you are transferred, use the following pretext:

"Dr. Noe completing medical papers for (the subject). Could you check the date of last treatment?" After the records clerk comes back to the phone you would then pump her for further information, such as the subject's address, employer, insurance company, etc.

This succeeds about seventy percent of the time. If you succeed in obtaining the desired information, get the clerk's name so you can ask for her personally if you need to call that hospital again.

If you are refused the information, simply hang up and call the Billing Department of the hospital. The Billing Department usually has the same information as Medical Records.

If the Billing Department turns you down also, then try both departments again. This time, at two or three in the morning. At this hour, the clerks handling things can often be bamboozled easier than the personnel during daytime hours.

PHONY AUTHORIZATION

To obtain medical records, some people go so far as to set up a bogus lawyer's office with a mail forwarding service. They then write for their "client's" medical records, forging the subject's name on an authorization. An authorization which has worked in the past appears below.

Of course, this ruse is completely illegal. But I have never heard of any hospital investigating the validity of any records request. If you use a mail forwarding outfit in a foreign country, there is nothing they can do about it, anyway.

MEDICAL AUTHORIZATION

St. Patrick Hospital
7007 Heavenly Way
Valhalla, AK   99999

Sirs:

    You are hereby authorized and directed to give to the LAW OFFICES OF MOE & LARRY, Ltd., Attorneys at Law, any and all information you may have regarding the condition of DONNA DOE, when under observation or treatment by you, including history, findings and diagnosis, examination of X-rays, copies of all medical reports and bills. A photocopy of this authorization shall be considered with the same force and effect as an original.

_____   _____
DONNA DOE   DATE

A legal authorization like this one should get you the subject's medical records without further hassles.

58

IN PERSON

Some investigators have been known to appear at the Medical Records department in person, dressed in white, with a stethoscope hanging around their neck. Reportedly, these investigators have had great success using this method.

SHADY NURSES

Yet another way to get medical records is to enlist the aid of a shady nurse or secretary in a doctor's office. Such people can easily call up the hospital for the information. If they are your friend, they may even help you for free.

There used to be a company that obtained medical records for insurance companies. This company was in the business from the late 60's to the middle 70's. They made millions obtaining medical reports. Maybe after reading this chapter, you can be the next medical records tycoon.

— 14 —

LICENSE PLATES

License plate information is not of much value in missing persons investigations. But you never know — the owners of cars parked near the subject's relatives and friends might be persuaded (perhaps monetarily) to discern the subject's location for you.

License plate records are open to the public in all 50 states and no ruse is needed to obtain them. When writing for these records, include the necessary fee and ask for an abstract of registration on the plate number.

Listed below are the bureaucratic agencies to write to for license plate records in all 50 states.

ALABAMA
Motor Vehicle and License Division
PO Box 104
3030 E. Boulevard
Montgomery, Alabama 36130
Fee: $0.25

ARKANSAS
Motor Vehicle Division
PO Box 1272
Little Rock, Arkansas 72203
Fee: $1.00

ALASKA
Division of Motor Vehicles
PO Box 960
Anchorage, Alaska 99510
Fee: $2.00

ARIZONA
Arizona Motor Vehicle Division
PO Box 2100
Phoenix, Arizona 85001
Fee: $1.00

CALIFORNIA
Dept. of Motor Vehicles
PO Box 11231
Sacramento, California 95813
Fee: $1.00

COLORADO
Dept. of Revenue
Motor Vehicle Master Files Section
140 W. 6th Avenue
Denver, Colorado 80204
Fee: $1.25

CONNECTICUT
Commissioner of Motor Vehicles
60 State Street
Wethersfield, Connecticut 06109
Fee: $0.50

DELAWARE
Motor Vehicle Division
Registration Section
PO Box 698
Dover, Delaware 19901
Fee: $2.00

DISTRICT OF COLUMBIA
Bureau of Motor Vehicles
301 C Street, NW
Washington, D.C. 20001
Fee: $0.50

FLORIDA
Dept. of Highway Safety and Motor Vehicles
Kirkman Building
Tallahassee, Florida 32301
Fee: $0.50

GEORGIA
Dept. of Revenue
Motor Vehicle Division
Trinity Washington Building
Atlanta, Georgia 30334
Fee: $0.50

HAWAII
Hawaii
Director of Finance
County of Hawaii
25 Apuni Street
Hilo, Hawaii 96720

Kauai
Director of Finance
County of Kauai
Lihue, Hawaii 06766

Maui
Director of Finance
County of Maui
Wailuku, Maui 96793

Oahu
Director of Finance
County of Honolulu
1455 S. Bertania
Honolulu, Hawaii 96814

No fee for any of the above

IDAHO
Motor Vehicle Division
Dept. of Law Enforcement
PO Box 34
Boise, Idaho 83731
Fee: $1.50

ILLINOIS
Secretary of State
2701 S. Dirksen Parkway
Springfield, Illinois 62756
Fee: $2.00

INDIANA
Bureau of Motor Vehicles, Room 314
State Office Building
Indianapolis, Indiana 46204
Fee: $1.00

IOWA
Dept. of Transportation
Office of Vehicle Registration
Lucas Building
Des Moines, Iowa 50319
Fee: $0.50

KANSAS
Division of Vehicles
Dept. of Revenue
State Office Building
Topeka, Kansas 66626
Fee: $1.00

KENTUCKY
Dept. of Justice
Bureau of State Police
State Office Building
Frankfort, Kentucky 40601
Fee: $1.00

LOUISIANA
Dept. of Public Safety
Vehicle Regulation Division
PO Box 66196
Baton Rouge, Louisiana 70896
Fee: $2.00

MAINE
Motor Vehicle Division
1 Child Street
Augusta, Maine 04333
Fee: $2.00

MARYLAND
Motor Vehicle Administration
6601 Richie Highway N.E.
Glen Burnie, Maryland 21062
Fee: $1.00

MASSACHUSETTS
Registry of Motor Vehicles
100 Nashua Street
Boston, Massachusetts 02114
Fee: $1.50

MICHIGAN
Dept. of State
Bureau of Driver and Vehicle Services
7064 Crowner Drive
Lansing, Michigan 48918
Fee: $4.00

MINNESOTA
Driver and Vehicle Services
Transportation Building
St. Paul, Minnesota 55155
Fee: $1.00

MISSISSIPPI
Motor Vehicle Comptroller
PO Box 1140
Jackson, Mississippi 39205
Fee: $1.00

MISSOURI
Dept. of Revenue
Motor Vehicle and Drivers Licensing Bureau
Jefferson City, Missouri 65101
Fee: $1.00

MONTANA
Dept. of Justice
Registrars Bureau
Motor Vehicle Division
Deer Lodge, Montana 59722
Fee: $2.00

NEBRASKA
Administrator of Titles and Registration
Dept. of Motor Vehicles
Capitol Building
Lincoln, Nebraska 68509
Fee: $0.75

NEVADA
Dept. of Motor Vehicles
555 Wright Way
Carson City, Nevada 89711
Fee: $1.50

NEW HAMPSHIRE
Motor Vehicles Division
85 Loudon
Concord, New Hampshire 03301
Fee: $3.50

NEW JERSEY
Division of Motor Vehicles
Bureau of Office Services
Certified Information Unit
25 South Montgomery Street
Trenton, New Jersey 08666
Fee: $5.00

NEW MEXICO
Motor Vehicle Division
Manual Lujan Sr. Building
Santa Fe, New Mexico 87503
Fee: $1.10

NEW YORK
Motor Vehicle Dept.
Registration Records Section
Empire State Plaza
Albany, New York 12228
Fee: $2.00

NORTH CAROLINA
Division of Motor Vehicles
Motor Vehicle Building
1100 New Bern Avenue
Raleigh, North Carolina 27611
Fee: $0.50

NORTH DAKOTA
Motor Vehicle Dept.
State Office Building
9th and Boulevard
Bismarck, North Dakota 58505
Fee: $0.50
Write for required form

OHIO
Bureau of Motor Vehicles
Correspondence Section — MVVRRC
PO Box 16520
Columbus, Ohio 43216
Fee: $0.50

OKLAHOMA
Oklahoma Tax Commission
Motor Vehicle Division
2501 N. Lincoln Blvd.
Oklahoma City, Oklahoma 73194
Fee: $1.00

OREGON
Motor Vehicle Division
1905 Lana Ave., N.E.
Salem, Oregon 97314
Fee: $1.00

PENNSYLVANIA
Dept. of Transportation
Motor Vehicle Bureau
Harrisburg, Pennsylvania 17122
Fee: $2.50

RHODE ISLAND
Registry of Motor Vehicles
State Office Building
Providence, Rhode Island 02903
Fee: $1.00

SOUTH CAROLINA
Dept. of Highways Public Transportation
Motor Vehicle Division
PO Box 1498
Columbia, South Carolina 29216
Fee: $1.00

SOUTH DAKOTA
Dept. of Public Safety
Division of Motor Vehicles

118 West Capitol
Pierre, South Dakota 57501
Fee: *None*

TENNESSEE
Motor Vehicle Division
Information Unit
Jackson Building
Nashville, Tennessee 37242
Fee: $0.50

TEXAS
Dept. of Highways and Public Transportation
Motor Vehicle Division
40th and Jackson
Austin, Texas 78779
Fee: $0.25

UTAH
Motor Vehicle Dept.
1095 Motor Ave.
Salt Lake City, Utah 84116
Fee: $1.50

VERMONT
Dept. of Motor Vehicles
Montpelier, Vermont 05603
Fee: $1.50

VIRGINIA
Division of Motor Vehicles
Box 27412
Richmond, Virginia 23269
Fee: $3.00

WASHINGTON
Vehicle Records
Dept. of Licensing
PO Box 9909
Olympia, Washington 98504
Fee: $2.00

WEST VIRGINIA
Division of Motor Vehicles
1800 Washington Street E.
Charleston, West Virginia 25305
Fee: $0.25
Write on business letterhead

WISCONSIN
Vehicle Files
Dept. of Transportation
PO Box 7909
Madison, Wisconsin 53707
Fee: $1.00

WYOMING
Motor Vehicle Division
2200 Carey Ave.
Cheyenne, Wyoming 82002
Fee: $1.00

OCCUPATIONAL
LICENSING BUREAUS

Check every city in which the subject is likely to be. These records are open to the public and no ruse is needed to obtain them.

STATE OF ILLINOIS

D R E **DEPARTMENT OF REGISTRATION AND EDUCATION**

320 West Washington—3rd Floor • Springfield, Illinois 62786 • (217) 785-0800
GARY L. CLAYTON—Director

December 20, 1983

Ronald G. Eriksen, II
▬▬▬▬▬

Dear Mr. Eriksen:

Department records reflect Paul ▬▬▬▬ address as
▬▬▬ ▬▬▬ Realty, Inc., 5227 ▬▬▬, Skokie, IL 60076.

If the Department of Registration and Education can be of further service to you, do not hesitate to contact the Licensure Maintenance Unit at 217/782-0452.

Sincerely,

Gary L. Clayton

Gary L. Clayton
Director

GLC:LS:bmz

When you write to a licensing agency about your subject, you'll probably get something like this back.

— 16 —

PHONE BOOKS AND CITY DIRECTORIES

Looking through phone books and city directories usually will not lead you to the person you are looking for. A person who knew someone was looking for them would have to be a drooling imbecile to have his name listed in such places.

Where phone books and city directories come in handy is finding people who know the person you are looking for. For example, phone books can be used to find people with similar surnames. These people just might be relatives. City directories can be used to find ex-neighbors.

Local city directories and phone books for major U.S. cities can be found in most public libraries.

I have found that the best city directories are put out by R.L. Polk and Cole Publications. These two companies operate much like the U.S. Census Bureau. They get their information by sending their people door to door to find out who lives where. Thus they are more complete than the directories put out by the phone company which only include people with published telephone numbers.

These directories usually cost around $100 a year. However, if you claim to be from a library which leases these directories, you can obtain information on almost any address in the country for free by calling the corporate headquarters of R.L. Polk at (313) 292-3200 or Cole at (402) 475-4591.

Old city directories can be found in the Library of Congress and in some historical societies. These old directories will come in handy for cases where an adoptee is looking for his biological parents.

POST OFFICE

It is possible that the person you are looking for may have been stupid enough to inform the post office of his new address. You can find out by sending $1.00 to his old post office and requesting his current address. When writing to any post office, always send your letter via registered mail. This will encourage the postmaster to reply in a reasonable amount of time.

A cheaper way to get the information is by sending a letter to the person's last known address with the words "Do Not Forward — Address Correction Requested." This will get you the information for free.

POST OFFICE BOXES

It's not hard to find out the street address of someone who has a post office box. It is reported that the following two telephone ruses have a 90% success rate.

RUSE 1

Post Office: Gila Bend post office.
Operative: Hi, this is Bob Bozo over at the State Attorney's office downtown. We have a grand jury summons here for a Betty Bovine

at Post Office Box six at your post office. We can't make service of process on a post office box; we have to give it to her personally. Do you have her street address?

Post Office: We can't give out that information over the phone.

Operative: Sir, this is official business. We have a deadline to meet on this. I'm sure you can understand.

Post Office: Just a minute. *Pause...*

Post Office: We've got her at 321 Baseline Road here in Gila Bend.

Operative: Thank you.

RUSE 2

Post Office: Gila Bend post office.

Operative: Hello, my name is Betty Bovine. I came in last week to close our post office box and have our mail sent here instead. The reason I'm calling is that we haven't received any mail this week. I'm wondering if there hasn't been a mixup somewhere.

Post Office: Hold on a minute, Mrs. Bovine. *Pause...*

Post Office: Mrs. Bovine, we don't have any record of you closing your box. In fact, there is mail in your box now.

Operative: You're kidding! That mail is supposed to be forwarded to me here. Do you have my address? What address do you have me at?

Post Office: It says here you're at 321

75

Baseline Road. Is that where you want your mail delivered?

Operative: Yes, would you do that please.

Another way to obtain the desired information is to call the post office and claim you have ordered some merchandise from the boxholder that was never received. Explain to the clerk that you would like the street address and telephone number so that you can complain personally to the boxholder.

SUBPOENAS

Subpoenas are handed out at the County Clerk's office. Simply pick one up and type in the appropriate information. Then take it to the post office and show it to the postmaster. Tell him that you have to serve it on the boxholder personally and that you need the street address. This scam has proven successful 100% of the time.

SMALL TOWNS

In small towns, postal employees will often know quite a bit about the person you are looking for. The mailman who handled the route where the subject used to live is an extremely valuable source of information.

The postal employees in these small towns are unbelievably friendly and will often go out of their way to help you. For example, I have had people actually look in the post office box of the person I was looking for and read off the addresses of the people who had sent him mail.

U.P.S. RUSE

On the off chance that a small town post office won't

IN THE CIRCUIT COURT FOR THE SIXTEENTH JUDICIAL CIRCUIT
KANE COUNTY, ILLINOIS

GEN. NO. _____

_____

VS.

_____   _____
PLAINTIFF(S)   DEFENDANT(S)

SUBPOENA

NOTICE TO ATTORNEY
Chapter 110 A, Section 204 requires the Clerk to issue Subpoenas on request, except that Subpoenas for discovery depositions of PHYSICIANS and SURGEONS may be issued only upon ORDER OF COURT. It also requires that the original be filed with the Clerk after service, with proper return thereon. Please comply by filing the WHITE COPY with the Clerk after service has been made.

NOTICE TO WITNESS
The attorney who has requested this Subpoena is listed herein. Any questions regarding your knowledge of the subject matter or testimony in the case at hand should be directed to him. As a further assistance to you, he has listed the location and room number where you are to appear.

Subpoena Directed To:
Name
Address
City   Zip

To Appear:
Date   Time
Room No.   Judge

To Speak In Behalf Of: ☐ Plaintiff ☐ Defendant
Name:

Attorney Name
Address
City   Zip
Phone

The People of the State of Illinois
TO THE SHERIFF OF KANE COUNTY:

GREETINGS:

   We command you to summon the person to whom this Subpoena is directed, to appear before the Circuit Court for the 16th Judicial Circuit, Kane County, Illinois, at the place and time indicated herein, to testify and to speak the truth on behalf of the party set forth, in a cause now pending in said Court.
   And have you then and there this writ, with a return hereon, showing in what manner you have executed the same.

   WITNESS, JAN CARLSON, Clerk of The Circuit Court, and the Seal thereof, at my office in Geneva, Illinois,

this _____ day of _____ 19___

Jan Carlson
Clerk of the Circuit Court

RETURN

I Certify that on _____ , 19___ I served this writ on the

within named _____ by leaving a copy with him/her personally and informing him/her
of its contents.

Fees — Service and Return .... $_____	Sheriff
Miles .... $_____	
Total .... $_____	By _____ Deputy

WHITE COPY — Clerk's Copy (To be returned by Sheriff or Attorney after Service.)
YELLOW COPY — Service Copy   PINK COPY — Attorney Office Copy

Subpoenas like this one are handed out at the County Clerk's and can help you get your subject's address.

give you the street address of someone who lives in their town, you can try the following telephone ruse.

Post Office: Cornland post office.

Operative: Hi, this is Bob Bozo calling from U.P.S. in Chicago. Our driver is at a pay phone in your town and needs directions to the Ginger Goodbody residence on Route One.

Post Office: Just a minute, I'll check our map. *Pause...*

Post Office: She's not on Route One. She's on Coon Road, three houses east of the railroad tracks. It's a little red house.

Operative: Thanks a lot.

— 18 —

SOCIAL SECURITY
RECORDS

The Social Security Administration is a gold mine of information for any investigator. The inquisitive people at Social Security keep tabs on where virtually every person in the United States lives and works.

Many investigators have contacts in the Social Security Administration whereby they can have a printout done on anyone's records. This usually costs the investigator around $15 per person checked.

The unfortunate thing about Social Security is that they are always at least three months behind in their records. Thus, these records do the investigator little good if the person he is looking for just took off.

Interestingly, the Social Security people have a department that will forward a letter to long-lost friends, relatives, neighbors, etc. They won't tell you the address of the person you are looking for — all they will do is forward a letter. The address of the department in Social Security that handles these matters is: Social Security Administration, Location Services, 6401 Security Blvd., Baltimore, MD 21235. When writing to this department, try to include as much information as you can about the person you are looking for.

The author is certain that some unethical people have taken advantage of the Location Services Department. It would not take much time or effort to send a letter to the person you are looking for through the Social Security Administration. In the letter, you could claim to be his long-lost illegitimate brother. Even if he was sure you couldn't possibly be related, he might call you (collect, hopefully) or write you a letter which contained his current address.

You can tell where someone first applied for their social security card by looking at the first three numbers. Here is a Social Security number prefix list to guide you in your search.

001-003	New Hampshire	362-386	Michigan
004-007	Maine	387-399	Wisconsin
008-009	Vermont	400-407	Kentucky
010-034	Massachusetts	408-415	Tennessee
035-039	Rhode Island	416-424	Alabama
040-049	Connecticut	425-428	Mississippi
050-134	New York	429-432	Arkansas
135-158	New Jersey	433-439	Louisiana
159-211	Pennsylvania	440-448	Oklahoma
212-220	Maryland	449-467	Texas
221-222	Delaware	468-477	Minnesota
223-231	Virginia	478-485	Iowa
232-236	West Virginia	486-500	Missouri
237-246	North Carolina	501-502	North Dakota
247-251	South Carolina	503-504	South Dakota
252-260	Georgia	505-508	Nebraska
261-267	Florida	509-515	Kansas
268-302	Ohio	516-517	Montana
303-317	Indiana	518-519	Idaho
318-361	Illinois	520	Wyoming

521-524	Colorado	540-544	Oregon
525	New Mexico	545-573	California
526-527	Arizona	574	Alaska
528-529	Utah	575-576	Hawaii
530	Nevada	577-579	Dist. of Columbia
531-539	Washington		

TELEPHONE RECORDS

The telephone records of the subject and his friends and relatives could give you valuable clues to his location. Maybe the subject called someone at his new location before he left. Or maybe one of his friends or relatives called him at his new location.

These kinds of records are easily obtained. All one need do is call up the telephone company service representative and pretend to be the person whose records you want. Tell her you never made any call to Missoula, Montana, and complain about being billed for it. Of course, she will tell you they have no record of any such call. At that point, you would ask what calls she does have a record for. She will then give you a listing of all numbers "you" called in the last month. This includes the numbers of people who called "you" collect.

C.N.A. NUMBERS

Once you have the toll records you need to find out to whom these records belong. Fortunately, Ma Bell has secret telephone numbers called "C.N.A. Service Numbers" which you call, give the number in question, and you will be told the name and usually the address which correspond with that number. The C.N.A. service numbers for various areas of the United States are listed below. As you would expect, the phone company does not want you to know about these. These numbers are good as of the first of 1984.

Telephone companies change their C.N.A. numbers at regular intervals. You can obtain the latest C.N.A. number by calling up the phone company in question and telling them you are from a different phone company and that you need the new C.N.A. number to settle a customer dispute.

Area Code	C.N.A. #	Area Code	C.N.A. #
201	676-7070	309	217-525-5800
202	384-9620	312	796-9600
205	988-7000	313	223-8690
206	382-5124	315	518-471-8111
208	303-293-2333	316	816-275-2782
209	415-543-6374	318	504-245-5330
212	518-471-8111	319	402-580-2255
214	464-7400	401	617-787-2750
215	412-633-5600	402	580-2255
216	614-464-2345	403	425-2651
217	525-5800	405	236-6121
218	402-580-2255	406	303-293-2333
301	534-1168	408	415-543-6374
302	412-633-5600	412	633-5600
303	293-2333	414	424-5690
304	344-8041	415	543-6374
307	303-293-2333	416	487-3641
308	402-580-2255	418	514-861-2635

Area Code	C.N.A. #	Area Code	C.N.A. #
419	614-464-2345	612	402-580-2255
501	405-236-6121	613	416-487-3641
502	583-2861	614	464-2345
503	241-3440	615	373-5791
504	245-5330	616	313-223-8690
505	303-293-2333	618	217-525-5800
506	657-3855	701	402-580-2255
507	402-580-2255	702	415-543-6374
512	828-2501	703	804-747-1411
513	614-464-2345	705	416-487-3641
515	402-580-2255	707	415-543-6374
516	518-471-8111	712	402-580-2255
517	313-223-8690	714	213-501-4144
518	471-8111	715	414-424-5690
519	416-487-3641	716	518-471-8111
601	961-8139	717	412-633-5600
602	303-293-2333	801	303-293-2333
603	617-787-2750	804	747-1411
604	432-2998	805	415-543-6374
605	402-580-2255	806	512-828-2501
606	502-583-2861	807	416-487-3641
607	518-471-8111	808	212-334-4336
608	837-1177	809	212-334-4336
609	201-676-7070	815	217-525-5800

An alternative to the C.N.A. numbers is to look up the number in a "criss-cross" directory. Several companies publish these; just look in the Yellow Pages under "directories." Many public libraries also have them.

If you don't have access to a C.N.A. number or a "criss-cross" directory, you can still find out to which area a phone number belongs. In the back of most telephone books, you will find a prefix-location directory. These at least will allow you to focus in on your subject's locale.

Another useful reference is the report entitled *Telephone Areas Serviced by Bell and Independent Companies in the United States* (NTIA Report 82-97). This report shows which telephone companies operate in which areas of the United States, complete with maps. The report is available from the U.S. Department of Commerce, National Telecommunications & Information Administration, Office of Policy Analysis and Development, Boulder, CO 80303.

INFORMANTS

It is not very hard to find an informant in the phone company. Just about every woman between the ages of 18 and 35 knows someone who is a telephone operator. Such operators are treated like dirt by the phone company and are paid little more than the minimum wage. They will almost always be receptive to any reasonable offer (say, $10 for each non-published telephone number and address).

There is a certain person in a certain city in the United States who works for Bell security. This certain person obtains telephone records for law enforcement agencies and private investigators throughout the country for $20. Maybe a friendly private eye or police officer can refer you to this person.

— 20 —

WELFARE ROLLS

These records are particularly valuable in cases where a mother has skipped with her child. Often the mother has taken off on a whim with no thought given to where she is going or how she is going to support herself and her child. When the money runs out and she still doesn't have a job, she will not hesitate to hop aboard the gravy train.

Surprisingly, these records are not open to the public, even though you, as a taxpayer, are footing the bill. To obtain these records, you will need an informant or you will have to use a ruse such as the one below.

Public Aid: Good Morning, Department of Public Aid.

Operative: Soundex, please.

Public Aid: One minute please. *Pause...*

Public Aid: Soundex, can I help you?

Operative: Hi, this is Bob Bozo over at the State Attorney's office downtown. We have a grand jury summons here for Debbie D. Deadbeat, date of birth January 4, 1955. We've been unable to locate her, but we understand she is on public aid. Can you check your records and see what address you have her at?

Public Aid: Sure, hold on a minute. *Pause...*

Public Aid: We've got her at 101 Easy Street, here in Dallas.

Operative: Thanks a lot. Have a nice day.

21

OTHER LEADS
TO CHECK OUT

GARBAGE

Poking through the subject's garbage and that of his friends and relatives is something you will never see television investigators doing.

Nevertheless, the potential rewards of this task outweigh the often odorous drawbacks. People throw all sorts of interesting things into the trash. You might get lucky and find a plane ticket receipt, a letter, or some other item that might lead you to the subject's location.

As you would imagine, this is not the most pleasant type of work. When doing this kind of work, it is recommended that you wear gloves and some type of mask to protect yourself from foul matter and noxious odors.

Garbage is considered legally abandoned property, so law enforcement types won't bother you for taking it.

Stealing garbage is also useful in background investigations. You would be amazed at what can be found in people's trash.

LABOR UNIONS

Labor unions are very protective of their members. Often they don't even cooperate with law enforcement agencies. The only ruse which has proven effective against these people is to claim that you are a doctor and that you must get in touch with the subject immediately due to an emergency in the family.

MILITARY PERSONNEL

Are you looking for someone whom you know is in the United States armed forces, but aren't sure where he is stationed?

In this case, all you have to do is send the subject's name (including his middle initial) and social security number, along with $2.85, to World Wide Locator, Fort Benjamin Harrison, Indiana 46216. They will reply with a letter stating where the subject is stationed.

PET LICENSE BUREAUS

It's a long shot, but some people have been located this way. Just call up the licensing bureau and tell them that you have found the subject's dog and that you would like the owner's address so that the mutt can be returned.

PROPERTY OWNERS

The property owner or the landlord of the subject's last known residence may be in possession of valuable information concerning the subject or his whereabouts.

If the subject skipped on the rent or left the place a mess, the property owner or landlord will bend over backwards to help you. For example, one landlord drove all over town for two days looking for an ex-tenant that we were both looking for. He found him, too.

You can find out who owns a particular piece of property through the local tax assessor's office.

SALVATION ARMY

The Salvation Army operates a bureau that searches for missing persons. While they don't do a particularly good job, it should be remembered that the Salvation Army operates a large number of missions and flophouses throughout the country.

If you have reason to believe that the person you are looking for is a bum, or derelict, you might want to contact the Salvation Army. Send your inquiries to "Salvation Army Missing Persons Service" at the following addresses:

Central Territory Headquarters: 860 N. Dearborn St., Chicago, IL 60610. (Covers these states: IL, IN, IA, KS, MI, MN, MO, NE, ND, SD, and WI.)

Eastern Territory Headquarters: 120 W. 14th St., New York, NY 10011. (Covers these states: CT, DE, ME, MA, NH, NJ, NY, OH, PA, VT, and RI.)

Southern Territory Headquarters: 1424 N.E. Expressway, Atlanta, GA 30329. (Covers these states: AL, AR, FL, GA, KY, LA, MD, MS, NC, OK, SC, TN, TX, VA, DC, and WV.)

Western Territory Headquarters: 30840 Hawthorne Boulevard, Rancho Palos Verdes, CA 90274. (Covers these states: AK, AZ, CA, CO, HI, ID, MT, NV, NM, UT, WA, and WY.)

TRAVEL AGENCIES, AIRLINES AND BUSES

If the subject has not departed yet, you can sometimes obtain desired information by posing as the subject and calling these companies up to reconfirm "your" reservations.

If the subject has already left, you will probably need an informant.

UTILITY COMPANIES

Utility companies are surprisingly good sources of information. People in lower economic classes often leave no paper trails such as drivers licenses, credit records or telephone records. However, many of these people are on record as being hooked up to their local utility companies.

I have never had any trouble getting information from water companies. Just call up or walk in and ask if the person you are looking for is hooked up.

Electric companies are more difficult to obtain information from, and you may need to use a ruse such as the State Attorney's scam mentioned earlier.

VOTERS REGISTRATION RECORDS

These records are particularly valuable in large cities. Politicians and other rabble rousers often run "get out the vote" campaigns and put relentless pressure on their constituents to register to vote.

I have been pleasantly surprised at how useful these records are. On more than one occasion, I have found such people as welfare recipients and skid-row bums through these records. These people are among the most difficult to find.

Voters registration records are public information everywhere. The only problem I have had with these records is that you have to go in person to get them. For some reason, the bureaucrats who handle these records refuse to give out the information over the phone.

22

CASE HISTORIES

CASE #1

The subject was a 30 year old white male who had skipped town, leaving a wife, four kids, and numerous bills. The subject's mother knew where her son was, but refused to reveal his whereabouts.

How Found. All usual tracing methods proved fruitless. The operative then had the subject's wife call her mother-in-law under the pretext that one of the children was deathly ill and needed a blood transfusion from the father. The mother-in-law was told to call her son immediately. When the conversation ended, the wife did not hang up. Instead, she played a tape recording of a dial tone through the telephone. While the mother-in-law was dialing her son's number, the wife used another tape recorder to tape the digits dialed. Using a tone decoding device (available from many "security electronics" dealers) the number dialed was decoded. The number turned out to be the subject's place of employment. Within 24 hours, the subject was served legal papers ordering him to appear in court. Later, his wages were garnished.

CASE #2

The subject was a 22 year old white female who had jumped bond on a retail theft charge.

How Found. Investigation revealed that the subject was a small-time dope dealer. Arrangements were made through local contacts to make a buy from her at a Little League field in another part of town. When the subject appeared, she was immediately brought into custody. Her boyfriend had to be "physically handled" to insure the operative's safety.

CASE #3

The subject was a 25 year old black male who had skipped out on a $5,000 loan.

How Found. It was discovered that the subject's drivers license had been transferred to Ohio. After determining the address on the Ohio license, the operative called the property owner to confirm that the subject still lived there. The property owner told him that the subject had been sent to state prison for several armed robberies.

Calling up the state prison and claiming to be from his local State Attorney's office, the operative learned that the subject had been released and that the prison didn't have his new address.

The subject's parole officer was then called. He informed the operative that the subject had finished his parole and had moved to a small town in Louisiana. Nobody with the subject's last name was listed with the information operator. The operative then called the local sheriff claiming to be a "special process server" with a summons for the subject. The sheriff was very familiar with the subject, but didn't know his address. The next day, the sheriff called with the subject's exact address and where he was employed. Later, a lien was put on the subject's property and his wages were garnished.

CASE #4

The subject was a 15 year old white female who had run off with her 35 year old boyfriend. The girl's parents were concerned about her safety and wanted her found.

How Found. Interviews with associates of the boyfriend revealed that the couple had probably gone to Odessa, Texas, to seek work. A check with all government bodies in Odessa brought forth the fact that the boyfriend's car had recently been ticketed for illegal parking.

The operative then proceeded to call every apartment, rooming house, trailer court, hotel and motel listed in the Odessa Yellow Pages.

This extremely boring task finally paid off when an apartment manager said that the couple was living in one of her units.

That night, the girl's parents flew to Odessa and brought their wayward daughter home.

CASE #5

The subject was a 29 year old black male who skipped out on a car loan. The finance company wanted the subject located so that the car could be repossessed.

How Found. Investigation revealed that the subject had been recently discharged from the U.S. Army. The operative then called the subject's mother claiming to be "Colonel Bill Stewart" from Fort Bragg, North Carolina. The mother was told that her son had failed to sign his discharge papers and that the Army needed to contact him immediately. The mother informed the operative that her son was living at the Antler Motel in Laramie, Wyoming, and that he was working for the U.S. Department of the Interior.

The operative then verified that the subject was still there by calling the Antler Motel.

Within seven days, the subject's car was repossessed by a local repo man.

CASE #6

The subject was a 30 year old white male who had skipped on a $7,000 loan.

How Found. The subject's ex-wife eagerly told the operative that the subject had gone to Houston, Texas, to seek work as a welder.

All usual tracing methods proved fruitless. An advertisement offering high-paying jobs for welders was then placed in Houston's leading newspaper. In the ad, prospective employees were directed to send in their resumes to a post office box in Houston.

Within three days, the operative received a resume from the subject which contained his new address.

— 23 —

THE FINAL WORD

To the uninformed, locating missing persons must seem like a terribly difficult task. But as you have seen, just about anybody can be easily found if you want to find them.

I leave you now with some words of wisdom that should prove inspiring when you are tracking down your prey. Good luck.

"They can run, but they can't hide."
— **Joe Louis**

"Everybody is somewhere."
— **Unknown**

"A monkey in a suit is still a monkey."
— **Emiliano Zapata**

"The glory of the deed lies in the finishing of it."
— **Genghis Khan**

RECOMMENDED READING

Good books on locating missing persons are hard to find. The only other books devoted solely to the subject are either incomplete and misleading or are occult type books which are of no value to clear thinking people.

The books listed below contain information which would be of genuine value to missing persons investigators.

The Private Investigator by Gene Blackwell, Security World Publishing, Los Angeles, CA, 1978. *This is the only good private investigator type manual. The section on in-person pretexts is very well done.*

The Muckraker's Manual by M. Harry, Loompanics Unlimited, Port Townsend, WA, 1984. *This book was written for investigative reporters, but many of the techniques in it are relevant to missing persons investigations.*

How to Get Anything On Anybody by Lee Lapin, Auburn Wolfe Publishing, San Francisco, CA, 1983. *This book carries a big price tag ($30.00) and its skip tracing section is incomplete. But it is the best book out on surveillance devices and techniques. You must get this book if you are a professional investigator.*

Search by Jane Askin, Harper & Row, New York, NY, 1982. *This is by far the best book for adoptees looking for their biological parents.*

Covert Surveillance & Electronic Penetration edited by William B. Moran, Loompanics Unlimited, 1983. *Contains chapters on shadowing and tailing methods, night vision devices, wiretapping, and body-mounted transmitters.*

How to Investigate Your Friends & Enemies by Louis Rose, Albion Press, St. Louis, MO, 1981. *Another good book on investigative reporting.*

The Big Brother Game by Scott French, Gnu Press, San Francisco, CA, 1975. *This book has been around for a while and is considered a classic. It covers investigations, bugging, surveillance and similar subjects.*

Directory of U.S. Mail Drops by Michael Hoy, Loompanics Unlimited, Port Townsend, WA, 1987. *Useful if you need a mail forwarding service to set up a phony lawyer's office or to operate a private investigation service out of state.*

Among the Missing by Jay Robert Nash, Simon and Schuster, New York, NY, 1978. *This book won't help you locate anyone, but it is fun to read on a rainy day. It contains interesting stories on people who have disappeared permanently.*

YOU WILL ALSO WANT TO READ:

——MP